# Are YOU in Here?

## Life Experiences:  We All Have Them

### WRITTEN BY:

### CAROL HART-PARKER

ISBN: 0-7596-5749-1

This book is printed on acid free paper.

Cover design by Priscilla Derriskson Bradberry

1stBooks - rev. 05/06/02

# Acknowledgements

**FBW & Associates, Inc.**
**Germantown, Ohio**
**Flonzie Brown-Wright, Consultant**

**Cover Design by:**
**Priscilla Derrickson-Bradberry**

*All photographs are the personal property of*
## Carol Hart-Parker
*838 E. Harrison Street*
*Danville, Ill 61832*
*(217) 442-6645*

**Special Friends who provided personal assistance:**

| | |
|---|---|
| *Charlene Puckett-Randle* | *Robert* |
| *Sondar Allison* | *Tracey* |
| *Denise "Niecy" Taylor* | *&* |
| *John S. Turner, III* | *Tara Parker-Blue* |

**Special Acknowledgements:**
*Lois Williams and Terry Ellis*

To God Be The Glory

Here's to your health!

May you, Greta Waddell, grasp every thing that God has for you, a wonderful life! Prosperity, health and love for each other. How wonderful it feels to be in your circle Family & friends.

Enjoy the poetry.

With Love & Respect

Carol Parker

8/3/2002

iv

# *Introduction*

*What exactly makes a person decide to write a book? In this case, a book of poetry. Not a book of prose, but writings that go on and on and on because of the joy of penning your experiences and thoughts.*

*Nothing in this book is fiction, all is very true, written to relax my mind and bring laughter and thought to you.*

*See! There I go again. I have to be very careful because it's so easy for me to rhyme.*

*I began years ago just having fun with people and putting crazy stuff to rhyme.*

*Our children, Tracey, Lantz and Tara have always been active culturally, therefore, paving the way for lots of writings.*

*Denise Taylor, my sister-in-law, really my sister, has provided me with many laughs whenever I said to her, "Aren't you 45 this year?" She would protest most profoundly by saying, "NO!!!" Well, finally after about five years of this, November 10, 1998 finally came when Denise turned 45, which prompted me to start writing this book.*

*That morning about 5:am, my eyes popped wide open as I thought..., Denise is really 45 today! I lay in bed rhyming things that I was going to finally be right in saying to her. I got up as not to disturb my husband, I went into the bathroom and began writing, "Happy Birthday, Niecy." I read it to her later that day and boy did she laugh. She, being a hard person to get to lauagh at a joke, caused me to know that it was alright to continue writing and so here is the first of how ever many you desire to read.*

### *Thank you and please enjoy!*

# Foreword

## "ARE YOU IN HERE?"

This collection of poems is like none other... It will tickle you... It will make you laugh out loud... If will have you reminiscing about the past... It will ultimately introduce you to Carol Parker, "One of the finest poetess of the new millennium".

So, sit up, read and enjoy, share the witticisms and chit-chat with friends and foe... after reading this book you know there will be more.

Love you girl,

*Terry Ellis*

## *Foreword, cont'd.*

On a beautiful holiday in a beautiful Illinois State Park, I had the opportunity to read Carol Hart-Parker's book of poetry entitled, "Are You In Here?" The poetry was absolutely delightful. I read the book from cover to cover in an afternoon.

Carol is so gifted she can capture any moment in life and transpose it to charming rhyme form. The book is appropriately named because you or I can relate to so much of it, from the death of a loved one as expressed in *"Sister"*, *"Our Gift at Christmas"*, to a snow blizzard in "January 1999."

I hope her poetry, which is just about every day situations, will bring you the joy it brought to me.

Lovingly,

*Lou Crockett*

## *Foreword, cont'd.*

"Are You In Here?"..., is a juicy slice of life that reaches into our past and pulls us into the present.

Through Carol's words, we can visit your family, whether gone on or here.

She has such vivid choice of words that she actually paints pictures with them.

"Are You In Here?", make you laugh, cry and remember the happy times.

It cleanses your soul with it earthiness.

Sisterly,

*Lois Williams*

*Foreword, cont'd.*

## To God be the Glory!

A song that expresses the life of
Mrs. Carol Hart-Parker.


Carol expresses the joys as well as the perils of
this life in a very unique way. Psalms 139:14 says
it best about Carol, *"I will praise you, for I am
fearfully and wonderfully made; marvelous are
your works."* And that my soul knows very well.

Carol is a very gifted poetess and singer. I can
Truly say, there is none like her.

After reading her poems, you will be filled with
different emotions. They will cause you to laugh
cry and even shout at the same time. To know
Carol is to love her, and to know all that she has
been through yet, see the smile that radiates from
her, will and does give you courage to go on a
little further. We can say for definite that what the
devil did for evil, God meant it for good!

So we salute you, Carol Hart-Parker..., This is
your season,

Your friends,

Leroy, Carol and Tiffany Shelton

## *"Three Hearts + One"*

In an effort to bring to life the stories contained in this work, I chose hearts to illustrate my "love" emotion. Being a mother and a sentimentalist, each color represents in a different way the connection between the love emotion I find in each of our children.

- ♥ **1st Heart** ~ *Best describes our daughter, Tracey. She is a precious ruby, a romanticist and one who possesses a very courageously spirit-filled character.*

- ♥ **2nd Heart** ~ *Best describes our son, Lantz. He was spiritually royal, passionate and straight forward.*

- ♥ **3rd Heart** ~ *Best describes our daughter, Tara. She is the essence of godliness, concern and sweet thoughtfulness.*

The fourth heart which is not displayed represents our grandson whom we are very sure will possess all the qualities of the three.

Love,

**Carol**

## *Editors Reflections….*

*Flonzie Brown-Wright*

*In July 1995, while visiting my parents in Mississippi, I met Carol and her husband, Robert. I invited them to come to a local bookstore that evening where I was autographing copies of my publication. I knew she would come. There was something in her eyes that spoke of honesty, excitement and curiosity.*

*When they came to the signing, as I gave her my "spill" about my publication, "Looking Back To Move Ahead", I felt that when the time was right, we would meet again. In my autograph to her, I expressed a hope for "future networking opportunities." More than four years later, my telephone rang with just that opportunity. Carol was calling to asked if I would assist her in bringing her long-held dream to fruition. With an excited and resounding **"YES"**, we began this project.*

*Carol, **THANK YOU** for choosing me to make this journey with you. I am pleased and thankful that this work and the potential of much more to come, will be all and more than you wish it to be.*

*Best wishes my Sister,*

# *Preface*
## 11/16/98


When first at these writings you take a look
No need to correct the grammar in this book,
It's all in fun though it's all very true
You might even find something in here that fits you.

I just wanted to share with you my life and time
To compile any experiences and put them to rhyme
There's been some uppers, there's been some downers
And yes I love making friend with all out of towners.

This started out being a book about health
But this life is too full to write of nothing else,
I hope when you read this it brightens your day
And push some of lifes problems out of your way.

So sit back, relax with that cup of tea
As you read and remember, yes that's happened to me,
Whether you're mother, father, grandparent or child
I hope while you're reading you're wearing a smile.

I'm a mother, and housewife that stays on the go
If you'd like to read more rhymes please write and let me know,
My post office number is on the back of this cover
Oh yes, did I mention I'm also a grandmother.

Hi Blue J.

# *"ARE YOU IN HERE?"*

*Carol Hart-Parker*

# The Guests
## 11/20/98

My house is a mess and I'm having guests
So I'll clean up some and hide the rest,
I guess I'll mix a lemon cake
I really hadn't planned to bake.

Let's see, I'll fix roast, macaroni and beans
Or should I fix Turkey, dressing and greens,
Why did I say dressing?
I know I can't make it
But I can buy box mix, that way I can fake it.

I must set my table with pizazz and flare
To show my dear friends how much we care,
We'll make them feel welcome, so they'll want to come back
I hope the next time it's just for a snack.

You see it was my idea to invite these folks
What they didn't know was it was only a joke,
I'm a New Woman, we don't cook anymore
After cooking for years it became such a chore.

When my husband and I shop for groceries and such
We don't buy a whole lot, it doesn't take much,
Since our children are gone and we're here by ourself
It's easier to open cans from the shelf.

Well I can't get out of it, it's too late now
Oh boy do I want to, but I don't know how,
Here they come, honey put on a smile
Oh know they brought houseshoes
Must be stayin' awhile.

# Bastin' In the Tub

After you've had a long day at work or play
And all you want to do is go home and lay,
When you're a child your have too's are small
But when you grow up you have to do it all.

You get home from work about ten after five
And before you know it six-o'clock has arrived,
You know your children have somewhere to go
So you gather them up and get the show on the road.

Lantz and Tracey to go rehearsal, Tara to ballet
To bad there's not 24 more hours in a day,
This is only Monday and you only have 4 more week days to go
Saturday there's a dance recital-Sunday there's a drama show.

You can hardly wait til the close of the day
When you can be alone
Without someone just dropping by
Or the ringing of the phone.

Your special moment is finally here
You're looking forward to a lotion rub
But there's nothing that will feel better
Than basting in the tub.

Dedicated to Denise

# Ode To Pork Meat

Goodbye to Pork Meat
Oh how I love you so
But you've filled my body full of worms
So now you've got to go.

I've loved you since I cut my teeth
I'll love you til the end
But not a piece of your poison meat
Shall pass my lips again.

I use to always tell my friends
There will always be pig on my breath
But since the Doc found parasites
I decided you won't cause my death.

# The Golden Rule

So you really honor The Golden Rule?
Even when bad things are done to you
It's not always easy, but very smart
To keep good feelings within your heart.

Respect is something that must be earned
Though many still have that to learn,
This life we live can spin your around
First lifting you up, then letting, you down.

I'd like to think that I'm a nice person
To be that way should take no rehearsin'
Let's all treat and greet people the same way
Although we sometimes may have a bad day.

Think of all the blessings that will come to you
If at first you practice The Golden Rule,
And if all this niceness is a problem
There's someone greater than us that will help you solve them.

# Laundry Madness

I went to the laundry to wash yesterday
School must have been out
Kids were all in my way.

Some with their mothers, some were alone
Others had stopped in to talk on the phone.

I checked all the washers and couldn't use one
So I took a seat until someone was done
One lady was finished, Halleyluyah I cried
Then her children brought seven more baskets inside.

Well back to my seat to wait my turn
Good thing I had all afternoon to burn
I waited and waited, I've been gone too long
My husband will surely think something is wrong.

These aren't the regular people that come in this place
I'm looking around can't recognize a face
They're looking at me like something is wrong
They're looking at me like I don't belong.

Kids were walking on washers and crawling on floors
And some even hanging on dryer doors
Where is the attendant I don't see her here
She's probably in the back tied to a chair.

I had an appointment I didn't want to be late
I looked at my watch and noticed the date
No wonder these people were all in my way
It's not Friday morning, It's Saturday.

*Carol Hart-Parker*

# Nothin To Do
11/21/98

It was Christmas Eve morning and under the house
Was my neighbors cat terrifying my pet mouse
My husband was trimming the tree in the yard
When the mailman delivered some Xmas cards

He stood in the doorway making small talk with me
Hoping he had a present under the tree
My daughter said what did you give him last year
I told her nothing now he has a pair

We were assembling, our annual cardboard fireplace
Securing it on the wall so it wouldn't fall on its face
We put thumb tacks in our tube socks and attached them to the top
So when weighed down with candy on the floor they wouldn't drop.

My husband was in the basement assembling a bike
I was upstairs bathing the tykes
The food was all cooked even sweet potato pie
The kids were in bed with their eyes opened wide

Bewitching hour had come their eyes were all closed
So shortly after old Santa arose
We hustled and scuffled to get all the toys in
And jumped into bed wearing a great big grin.

What happened the next day, stuff was everywhere
Even the clothes we had bought were thrown over the chair
All of their toys will occupy their time for a year
Hopefully til Christmas once again will appear.

One more Christmas this war was won
Now let's settle down and have some fun
I'm sitting back and trying to be cool
When my kids say to me
"Mommy I'm bored, there's nothing to do."

## Straighten Up and Fly Right

Now I know a lady and it's really not me
This lady is as mean as mean can be,
Her husband's a good man, works from seven til four
But she's all over him, soon as he hits the door.

She complains and fusses from the time he gets home
She better be careful, might cause him to roam,
He says to her, "What did I do wrong now?"
She said I'll think of something just give me a while.

I tell you this man is at home all the time
If he goes out anywhere he's home by nine,
Now there are SOME men on whom you can't depend
If she plays her cards right he'll be there til the end.

Problems occur you need each other to solve them
Hollering and screaming just won't resolve them,
I offered this solution she said she would take it
I think the lady and her man's gonna make it.

9

## *"ARE YOU IN HERE?"*

*Carol Hart-Parker*

# Please, Men, Get Serious

My mother told me something a long time ago.
She said come here and talk to me,
There's something you should know.

Some women feel they need a man,
That simply is not true.
Although the world is full of them,
That will be good to you.

You know men speak of P.M.S.
in many books you read.
But, what they fail to mention
is just what plants the seed.

Some say it's a chemical imbalance,
Some say women get it before their friend.
Most times the mood is over
When their friend's stay finally ends.

But ladies are not along in this,
This darkness and sometimes despair
for we all have changes we go through,
If you look you'll find them there.

Now, what prompted her to have this talk with me
Was to make me aware of changes in men
That they often fail to see.

One minute when you talk to some men
Their up—the next minute their down.
Who knows the next time you look at them
Their heads could be spinning around.

You won't know when it will happen
You may not have your guard up.
All you know is you ask a question
And they answer you abrupt.

Now, if you take a survey
Of all our precious men,
You'll find the reply, oh, no, not us!
Again and again and again.

I've been shown that men do have P.M.S.
And yes, their moods get bad.
So, yes, they all have periods,
They just don't have to wear pads.

# January 1999

I woke up this morning to a beautiful sight,
Everything outside had been draped overnight.
The first snow of the year, January 1999.
So, we toasted it in with our own special wine.

Now, you'd think with everything being covered with snow
You could make snow angels and a sledding you'd go.
Well, we're all dressed now with snowsuit and gloves
To go play outside with the people we love.

We go outside and what to our surprise
The snow out here is up to our thighs
We must find someone that has a truck,
We call all over town without any luck.

Mercy, how can we make it to the store,
We barely made it through the door.
The trees are all covered with snow and ice
All of a sudden, this doesn't seem so nice.

A little boy yells, "Can I clean your driveway?
I'll shovel it, but I can't haul it today."
We haven't had a snow like this in years,
Could be a celebration cause the 1900's end here.

The stores are all closed, the restaurants shut down,
There's not a soul stirring in our little town.
Let's go inside, this stuff is too deep.
We're covered from head to toe and looking like sheep.

We should have gone grocery shopping yesterday,
Cause all of the leftovers have been thrown away.
What shall we eat, what shall we do?
We'll eat syrup sandwiches, like we used to.

*Carol Hart-Parker*

Enough is enough, I'm ready to eat,
So, I sprang from the couch and onto my feet.
I'll pretend I have roast, but I guess I'll have toast.
In my mind I'll imagine which one I like most.

Rob's getting restless, he'd like to go down town.
And Gary's still asking, "Is it still comin' down?
Faye's wrapped in her blankets and snuggled up tight.
I'm walking back and forth looking for something to bite.

Well, so much for going out in this weather,
Maybe next time we'll be more prepared and together

# Old Food/New Food

I think I'll buy a farm cause food is too high
Today I paid for groceries and I thought that I would die

A loaf of bread now costs two dollars
Now that's enough to make you holler.

I looked for some corn, finally found some ears
They looked like they had been in that bin for years
What happened to the plump ears they use to grow
These look like they should've been fed to the crows.

My grandparents had the tastiest chicken around
Now they're all shot up with steroids and their feet don't touch the ground
Most cereal is five dollars now
And milk is so high you'd be better off buying a cow.

Don't mention the fruit all shrunken and tight
Better be prepared to scream if you try to take a bite
I used to buy potato chips that were full to the top
But buy some now, You guessed it half way up and they stop.

Well I'm not even going to get started on meat
To find a good piece would be such a treat
We have to eat, It's just that way
Perhaps we'll get our old food back someday.

# Too Young
## (The First Time)
### 11/19/98

Once I was married a long time ago
Why I did that awful thing, I will never know
Marriage is a wonderful union
A guidance from above.
Now that I think of it
What I felt wasn't really love.

The man (and I use the word loosely)
Kept me hungry and you see, I like to eat.
The biggest miracle that ever occurred
Is that we had shoes on our feet.

We lived with relatives
And their house was always cold.
When I woke up in the morning
My bones felt one hundred years old.

We didn't have a refrigirator to keep food in,
So, we kept it outside in a storage bin.
When I married my name became?_____.
My maiden name was Hart
To think the two sounded good together
Wasn't very smart.

Thank goodness all that garbage is in the bin
And I have been blessed with a wonderful man.
Although I like clowning, I still can act good.
My husband promised to stay as long as he could.

And now he looks at me and wonders what he's done,
All because he doesn't understand the prize I've won.
So, before you're aroused about a man and his name
Arm yourself, get ready, he may be playin a game.

# Our Gift at Christmas
## 11/17

What does Christmas mean to me
It's more than just a Christmas tree,
We buy special gifts and stuff
But that alone is not enough.

We decorate our entire house
Some even decorate cars,
Without even taking a moment
To thank our lucky stars.

They say December 25 is not that special day
They sat it's in the spring, how do we know anyway,
It seems to me what matters is that Jesus Christ was born
Whether it be springtime or one wintery morn.

I count my blessings everyday
That Jesus let me come this way,
To do the right things I knew I could
And live my life as I know I should,
Do we realize whose birthday this is
It is not ours, it's only his.

So when we find ourself slipping
And not doing what is right
You know that he will help us
If we try with all our might.

On Christmas let's thank God above
For the wonderful gift he gave us with love,
So let's all remember to celebrate
What happened to us on this wonderful date.

# *"ARE YOU IN HERE?"*

*Carol Hart-Parker*

22

# Ladies Who Have Thought of Suicide, But Won't
### 1/8/99

You know this is a hard world we live in today
Only liquor and drugs seem to get their way,
Sometimes remaining a lady seems to be such a chore
With society always demanding more.

When you get caught in a net as we sometimes do
And don't fight your way out cause you feel like you're through,
If only you were given a fraction of a chance
And not forced to others tunes to dance.

I'm so tired of food stamps and link cards
I want a Visa, to which I can charge,
The jobs I apply for takes a degree
So needless to say that doesn't apply to me.

I have four children with no husband in sight
And yes I love the Lord with all my might,
My mistakes I am paying for in more than one way
If I remain strong It will work out one day.

Hurray, Hurray in my mail today
Was a letter marked approved, my grant's on its way,
I want a gold tassel on my graduation hat
So I'll pray, study and parent, that will take care of that.

You know there were times when I was depressed
Not sure of what to do, my life was a mess,
But now things are much better, why wouldn't they be
Cause I let the Lord guide instead of me leading me.

Prove the world wrong, be a statistic? Don't.
This message is for
Ladies Who Have Thought of Suicide, But Won't.

*Carol Hart-Parker*

## *SPECIAL LADIES*

*Front Row~Pam, Charlene, Regina*
*Back Row~Aleta, Jackie, Carol, Bernica*

# Rob

I'd never find enough words to write about this man,
But the one thing that I'm sure of is that I'm h is biggest fan.
He is the kind of man that parents raised long ago.
Where you'll find another like him, tell me, I would like to know.

He loves anything to do with outdoors.
You can look out any window and see him doing chores.
He digs, plants, brows, and rakes, but never a lunch hour does he take.
He's Grandpa to our Blue J, who runs him raggedy the entire day.

He grows bananas and he makes wine.
When he puts on those suits, he looks so fine.
Now, if you need him to be your friend,
He'll be there for you again and again.

He's been my real friend since we were small children.
Together we caught lightening bugs, but never did we kill them.
I was five and he was eight,
I guess we knew then together we'd be great.

We've been together for thirty-four years.
I wouldn't leave him now if he begged me to with tears.
Knowing that he feels the same about me
Makes our love so special because on most things we agree.

Yes, he's a good man, I'll love him always.
It's with him I'll spend the rest of my days.

# Dear Tracey,

I love you, you're a friend of mine.
I keep thinking of how you keep me smiling all the time.
Now that you've been around the world more than twice
Did you find the people you encountered very nice?

Surely if they heard you sing
They'd want you to come back again.
I know you delighted them with your humorous way
And kept joy during all those days.

I wish that we could see you more.
You travel so far away.
But, believe me, you are in our prayers
Every hour of everyday.

When you were just a little girl
We know that we were blessed
To have you placed in our family
We know we had to do our best.

Well, tootale totalot, old goats like to trot.
The above quote is personal, you see,
Just between Tracey and me.
I know you still look marvelous,
I'm sure you will agree.
So, come on back to Danville, so we can all see

You are like the dandelion, all pretty and bright with a smile that shines.
But, once you've visited a place for a while, it's off to another to share that smile.
Like the dandelion when blown through he weeds
Everywhere you've been you've left some seeds.

*Carol Hart-Parker*

# Tara and Co.

Where do I begin about Tara and her friends
They drove me crazy from beginning to end,
She's going to a party, "Do I look alright?"
Oh Yeah!  Mamma can I stay all night?

Now who's having a slumber party this time
Don't forget your dance lessons tomorrow at nine,
She's a sweet girl never gave us problems
If she had any small ones then she would solve them.

Her personality is charming, her voice is quite blessed
When you hear her sing, you'll place her with the best,
Well high school is over, she's off to college
We hope she returns with a head full of knowledge.

Now Tara is married with husband and child
In the summer her little boy visits awhile,
When they come home our house is full
It makes me remember when she was in school

Growing up her co-partners were Donna, Tilnetta and Michelle
Also her cousin Reese and Danielle,
They are all gone now and I miss them so much
But I'm really lucky they all keep in touch.

*Carol Hart-Parker*

# Lantz

Dear Son, We miss you even though you're always near
Thoughts of you grow dearer from year to year to year
I hope you can use all the talents you had while here on earth
It was easy to tell you were chocked full the moment I gave birth.

As I see new inventions on the market today
I think of myself Lantz could have done that,
if only he hadn't gone away
We hope that you're happy we know that you're safe
I just want you there waiting when I open the gate.

Love, Your Family
1964-1995

31

# *"ARE YOU IN HERE?*

*Carol Hart-Parker*

# Tara and Ken = K.J.

We were in the labor room on that wonderful morn
The morning our beautiful grandson was born
Ken was right there with Tara, helping her through
We were at the foot of the bed not knowing what to do.

Her father rubbed her feet, I wiped her brow
Both anxiously waiting the birth of their child
Her tolerance was awesome, her bravery unshaken
I must say by the whole thing I was quite taken.

It was the most amazing thing I'd seen in my life
I think my son-in-law has a wonderful wife
We took pictures of the blessed event
We can't explain what being there meant.

I had caesareans so this was all new to me
So much pain to have a baby
Lets pay homage to all women
Who add to their family again and again

I think every person should at least once watch a birth
Perhaps we'd have better attitudes here on earth
How did God know what this would mean to me
Not a more beautiful sight shall I ever see.

You should see them with this baby
They are at his beck and call
I can tell they'll be good parents
By the way they handle him while he's small.

# The Only Grandchild

Our little K.J. is our pride and joy
And please believe us when we say he's all boy
He is the only grandchild we've got
We always thought that we'd have a lot.

He goes to a Christian School, I think that that is good
It will help him to grow to be that man that he should
He's a charming little boy, who will win your heart
And have you jumping through hoops right from the start.

We went to visit K.J. just two weeks ago
Where he gets his energy we will never know
His agenda is rigid and very full
In order to play his games you must follow his rules.

He explains how he wants it and makes it clear for you to see
We must adhere to his directions cause he's grown, he's almost three
There's a time out chair in case he doesn't act as he should
When he has to be seated he vows, "I'll be good."

We tell him he's a good boy that tries naughty things
To call him bad could injure his esteem
He wants to do everything for himself
But when he tries of trying he will ask for help.

He ran to his mommy the other day, reached up and kissed her
If I'm not mistaken, I think he asked he for a sister.

## I Do

There's a wedding in our family
Where do I begin
My husband and I are getting married again,
We married thirty years ago
Oh how I loved him then
I'd wed my sweetheart every year
For my love will never end.

I know he feels the same way
Cause he's so very good to me
I think he's one of the boldest leafs
On our family tree.

Together we've raised children
Paid for a house and cars
Enjoy sharing with others
Everything that we call ours.

So as we repeat our vows
And continue to share our love
We hope that all the things we do
Is smiled on from above.

# My Sister
## 11/19/98

Where's my sister Gail
Why isn't she here with me
That have fallen from our family tree
To know her was to love her
She was such a joy and delight
But Jesus took her to be with him one February night.

I can't explain how it feels to lose
A precious sister
I only know it hurts real bad when
I think of how I miss her.

You know we all have problems
And some can overcome
But we have to fight the battle
Until the war is won.

Sometimes I start to call her
I've even picked up the phone
And that is when I realized
She's not at her earthly home.

She was my little sister, but
She said I acted like her mother
Yes I watched her very closely
Cause I didn't have another.

When growing up we shared a room
We even shared some chores
When I think of all the things we shared
I miss her even more.

I love You Gail…

*Carol Hart-Parker*

# Jenea and Jeff

We love you, you will always be in our hearts
It could never be any different
Because we have loved you from the start.

# Morefield – Uncles, Aunts, & Cousins

Uncle Jim & Aunt Ollie have a daughter named Susan.
Let's see, is she ___ or ___? Sometimes age is confusion.
Susan is a school teacher, and cute as can be.

Uncle Bill has five children, 3 girls and 2 boys.
Boy, would I hate to buy those X-mas toys.
Let's see, there's Patsy, she's an artist.
And would probably say that she is the smartest.

Then there's Elroy, who can rebuild a car.
If he keeps up the good work, he'll ready go far.
Now, June, she's a dentist with all kinds of tools.
She should be a good one, June did you go to school?

Their sister is Tonya, who studied as she should,
Now she's a mortician, so you'd better be good.
Hey, Hey, Billy Kool-Aid's his nickname.
He's now in Minnesota seeking fortune and fame.
We Miss you Marty!

Uncle Buck has 5 children, he's not here anymore.
Some family members must go on before.
There's two in California, Claudie and Jeanette.
Claudie has been in the armed forces for so many years,
He looks so much like Papa except for the years.
Jeanette is a nurse out California way.
Treat her nice, I might need her one day.
Now, where is Willie, haven't seen him in a year.
I'll turn around one day and he'll be standing here.

Their mother is Aunt Dorothy, haven't seen her in a while.
She was always nice to me when I was a child.
There are two more sons, Carlos and Bryan.
Jan's a great mother. Boy, is she tryin'.
Carlos is probably startin' to feel his oats,
But he was wonderful manner that counts the most.
Bryan has opened up, he wouldn't talk much,
You were lucky if he'd even let you touch.
He'll talk with you one to another
And he loves to play basketball with his brother.

There was Uncle John, but he's gone you see.
Another gold leaf on our family tree.

Hey, Uncle Walter, tell me what ya know.
I know you know somethin', cause you told me so.
Respect to: Aunt Mayola.

Yo! Aunt Gladys—
Now, this is my mother's sister on the Morefield side.
You think that you can get away with
Something, but from her you cannot hide.
There's Greg, now, he's the oldest.
What it means is he keep his eyes on the others.
O.K., we come to Gary, he's really very kind,
Cause every time he sees me he says that I am fine.
Now, Mr. Curt, what does he do?
He goes to work, work, work, and plus he goes to school.
Curt's twin brother, Chris, is just a big ole clown.
I can't remember ever seeing his face weaving a frown.
The only girl, Patricia, is as sweet as she can be.
A true Christian, a loving cousin, that's very special to me.

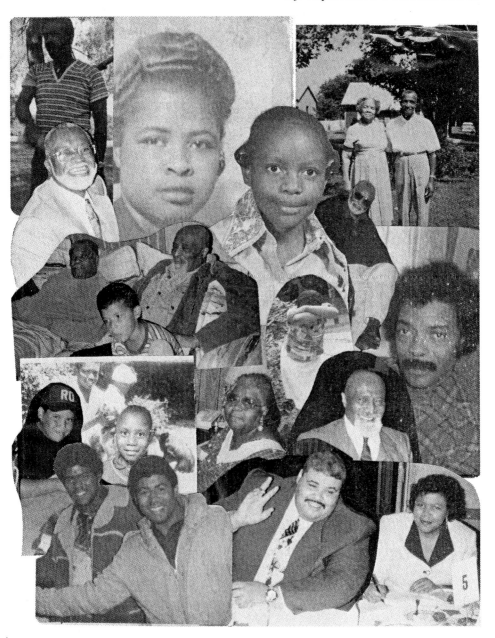

45

*Carol Hart-Parker*

# *"ARE YOU IN HERE?"*

*Carol Hart-Parker*

## Cousins on My Daddy's Side

Everyone has cousins, let's see where do I start?
There are two in California, Eric and Crazy Mark.
There's one in Arizona, his name is Harvey Eugene,
If you every have a party he and Mark
Should be on the scene.

There are five in Chicago, we don't see them much.
I'd really like to see them, I wish they'd get in touch.
There's Derk, Danere, and Drake, Johnny and Reginald.
I'd really like to see them before they all go bald.

Eric and Mark have a brother, we call him Little Luke,
But his name is really Luther, and I think he's kinda cute.
We see Luke every other month,
He even stayed two hours once.

In Atlanta there's Maria and Sharon.
They both are really very caring.
Sharon's kinda quiet, Maria is not.
If you hang with Maria, you'll really learn a lot.

Darrell is the minister on our family tree,
He'll help you through your problems,
I know, he's helped me.

Ellis (Pee Wee) has the music just for you.
Anything you want to hear, old or new.
He'll even make a tape of the O'Jays or the Topps,
There is no end to where his collection stops.

Boy, is Ronald crazy, as crazy as can be,
I never know what to expect he's going to do to me.
Put him in a kitchen, and wow, can that man cook.
Don't be surprised if you come across his recipes in a book.

Then there is Suzanne, she's a good cook, too.
So good she's written a cook book, just for you.
We all miss Tacky, his name is really Larry.
When it's time for our reward, with him we will be.
He's earned his gold leaf on our family tree.
He's kept us in stitches with the things that he's done,
Things that he's done probably since he was one (1).

Let's not forget Cedric.
He's the working man
He'll work as many hours as he can.
We don't see him much,
Til he rests when his shift is through,
But, he'll do anything that he can for you.

We come to Harvetta, now what can I say?
She is the same person from day to day.
She won't bite her tongue, she'll tell you what's true,
Including exactly what she thinks of you.

Now, there is Faye, I saved her til last.
Together we've shared so much of the past.
We call her phony, but she's for real,
Cause she will also tell you just how she feels.
This girl has made us laugh so much,
No wonder we've always kept in touch.
She's just so dramatic, you gotta lover her,
Find another like Faye, there is no other.

These are the cousins on one side of our tree.
I'm not sure, so you'll have to ask them
What they think of me.

Toodles

*Carol Hart-Parker*

# *"ARE YOU IN HERE?*

53

*Carol Hart-Parker*

# Aunt Ilena...

We have an aunt in Chicago, her name is Aunt Ilena
It's been ten whole months since we've last seen her.
When we get together we have so much fun.
Aunt Ilena brings laughter to everyone.

She has two children, Steven and Sandy.
She has four grandsons, Vincent, Daryl, Steven, and Danny.
These children are all grown, so that makes them men now.
How'd the years slip away, they'll have children after while.

Aunt Lena will always write you a line,
But I don't remember her using stationery one time.
She writes on order forms, grocery bills, or sacks.
She doesn't care what you use, as long as you write her back.

She says she is moving to Danville someday,
I won't wait at the state line
'Cause I'll probably look like Rip Van Winkle
By the time she makes up her mind.

Now, where does this leave Uncle James? (Protocol)
I bet he's going to move too.
You know he wouldn't stay in Chicago
If he couldn't look at you!

Love you, Aunt Lena...Carol

## Happy Birthday Niecy

Denise, you're forty-five today.
Oh, how the years have slipped away.
You cannot tell me anymore
Oh, no, no, no, I'm thirty-four.

Gone, gone, gone, just five more years to play,
Cause you'll be hitting fifty one day
And when you hit it, it will hit you right back
And knock you down and snap your neck.

So, run and jump and kick your heels
Cause fifty fills your cabinets with pills.
Your arms start hurting, you legs won't work.
This whole change will make you feel like a jerk.

You know the sliding board you played on as a tyke,
That's what getting old is like.
You go up slow and can party all night,
But after you reach the top you come down looking a fright.

If you don't believe me just look around,
And notice all the crooked-over people in this town.
They looked like you when they were forty-five
But, they didn't feel so swell when fifty arrived.

**(Happy Birthday Niecy continued)**

Now some slipped through the cracks and are doing fine,
But, here I stand with this broke knee of mine.

    I couldn't get through the cracks, but
      that's O.K.
     I'm sure I'll quit tippin' like a wolf
     someday.
     So, I'm just doing for you
      What no one else did for me
       And that's letting you know what happens at fifty.
       Did I see you grab your hip the other day?
       Well, you're just forty-five, it'll go away.

       But not too far, it's just waiting in the wings
       Cause five more years it will be
       back again.
       Now, remember all I've said and
       pass it on
      Soon your gonna wonder where those
      non-aching years have gone.

Well, I got to go and take some pills,
I'll meet you at the drugstore at the top of the hill
And we'll roll down together, cause walkin's unreal.
Love, Mrs. Parker, III

# Happy Birthday Aunt "Blue Eyes"

Now here's a lady I must tell you about
She will keep you laughing until you fall out,
She's my father's sister
She left town and we missed her,
But she returned, cause for us she yearned.

When I was little she'd come to our house
To hear everything, she said I was quiet as a mouse,
She'd bring with her Eugene and Faye
Cause she had come to spend the day.

She had a pet name for us to call her
If we did not do it she would not answer,
Her name is Aunt Helen, but-
She said if we were wise, Instead of Aunt Helen
We should call her Aunt Blue Eyes.

So that's what we called her
From that day to this
To call her anything else would be remiss.

Now that we're older we still call her Blue Eyes
But she tells us not to and we don't know why,
Today is her Birthday which name shall I use
As I sing Happy Birthday I'll let her choose.

*Carol Hart-Parker*

# Happy Birthday Claudette

I call and tell you happy birthday every time
One of these years you're gonna remember mine,
I hope you get a lot of presents
Eat a lot of pheasant
And have a lot of fun when it's holiday time.

I know you don't live around me anymore
But that ain't no reason to close the door,
You never call me up
I don't see you much,

What's wrong with ya girl
Why don't cha keep in touch.
Now I hope you have fun, on your speical day
Now that you got my call, you can be on your way.

Girl I probably won't see ya til summertime
Unless you drop by to drink some wine,
Don't forget to tell Donald I said Hi
So long, see ya later, farewell, bye-bye.

You call me now, It took long enough
Both of us are old enough to be dipping snuff,
But I look forward to your call on my birthday
Which proves just wait, things will come your way.

## Sister of Mine (Ours) Ernestine

I just can't help but write about
My sister in Christ, Ernistine
No matter how long I make this tribute
I can't explain what her love and friendship means.

I've known her for quite a while
Never once seeing her without a smile,
She's a person on whom you can depend
Don't sorry cause she'll work and won't stop til the end.

She's helped my family in many ways
In many ways we simply can't repay,
If you ask her why she works so hard
She'll respond by saying "I love the Lord."

It's not just in church that her caring shows
Being there for family, friends, community is all she knows,
As folks read this poem
There are some who just might say
I remember wrong she's done back in the day.

But those things aren't important
She's been forgiven, so they're dead and gone
It just might be those things that made her weak
Are the same things that made her strong
All I ask is that she doesn't change, that I'm sure I won't
see
So now I'd like to honor her
With love from you and me.


Ernie I love you!
Love,
Carol 1-17-99

# *"ARE YOU IN HERE?"*

# Family Tree

You know I love my family
They mean the world to me
But we all probably have some strange fruit
Growing from our family tree.

And since I'm in control of this poem
I guess I'll start with me
Cause my family says I'm the strangest fruit
That ever burdened a tree.

You see I love to have my fun
Tomorrow's not promised to anyone,
So I'll dress in costume and go all over town
It's all in fun though it's all very true
And yes, I'll also dress up as a circus clown.

Are you the joke on your family scene
If you are then you know exactly what I mean,
I even have a party dress
In which they say I look a mess.

I have an Aunt Mary, She loves that dress so
Whenever there's a family party, I wear it and put on a show,
This was supposed to be about my family
But as you see it turned out to be about me,
So I'll write another and pay homage to my wonderful family.

*Carol Hart-Parker*

## Our Children
11/18/98

Do you have children?  I have three
One is no longer here with me
He's gone ahead to his special place
When its time we'll be blessed to see his face.

If you have children as some of us do
Then you'll know they only depend on you
Be careful the way you raise them these days
With love and respect in hopes they wont stray.

You know, some things have changed, they're not like before
The respect we deserve is not there anymore
Of course we can't say that all kids are the same
Some prefer to stay back, others go on to fame.

Let's see where do we start, what shall we do?
The discipline should start before they are two
Beginning that early should not be a chore
Manners can be developed before they are four.

You must do things with them, to show that you care
So it will be imbedded that you'll always be there
As they grow up as we know they do
Remember they won't always be living with you.

Just think when you know that you've done your best
And it's time for the world to give them their test
Always be available to give advice
Because they will ask for it more than twice
Sometimes you'll be wondering what they're doing, where they are
But away from your heart, they're not very far.

*Carol Hart-Parker*

68

*Carol Hart-Parker*

# Grandparents
## (um, um, the best)

# Grandparents (um um the best)

Now just who thought of grandparents, I know I'm glad they did
Otherwise who would've been our refuge when we were only kids
Do they give you what you ask for – you know they always try
Even if they have to sneak it to you and be very sly.

How do you explain them?  There is no way
You just know everyday you are around is your day
If I could jump through hoops or even fly in space
I know that I would do it just to watch his face.

Grandparents are there to say yes when parents say no
We know that we shouldn't but that's just the way it goes
I'll say we have to work on this, we really don't want to win
Because I make sure my mouth stay shut when the discipline begins.

We Love You Grandbabies

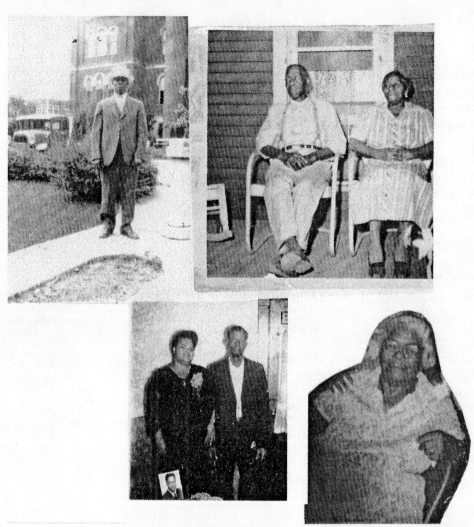

*Carol Hart-Parker*

# Dear Lois

No matter when I need you
Without me looking, you're always there
Whatever the situation
You always show me that you care.

A true friend is a blessing
That is sent from up above
You don't always have to be around them
To know that you are loved.

So daily I count my blessings
And among them I place you
Because of all the people I have encountered
There have not been many that measure up to you.

With all the uncertainties
There's one thing of which I'm very sure
Our friendship is a blessed one
That's clean and bright and pure.

Wishing you the most wonderful of any birthday
Love,
Carol

# *"ARE YOU IN HERE?"*

*Carol Hart-Parker*

# Girlfriends

Thank you so much for your thoughtfulness and caring
Thanks for your love, your prayers and your sharing,
It all means so much to the spirit and the mind
To have friends like you who to me are so kind

# lark to go in first round

## Congrats Keon

In our town there's a young man named
Keon
A basketball star, I knew he'd be one.
When I subbed at the High School
He'd walk in all cool
And say "I've lot my seat, may I have a new
one?"

He really loved to play and fool around
But he never exchanged words when I said
"Keon sit down."
He had manners then as he has now
To me his mother has raised an honorable
child.
As he continues to be a role model for kids
everywhere
It allows kids to say WOW! I can go there.
But first you must study and make the
grades
Cause when the ball stops bouncing you still
gotta get paid.

*Carol Hart-Parker*

# College at 52!

I went back to college at age fifty-two
It seems that I had nothing better to do,
Our children are grown and out on their own
Leaving my husband and me here all alone.

Let's see what classes I should sign up for
I'd better just takes three, though I'd rather take more,
What three should that be for someone old as me
It's certain that one of them won't be P.E.

Come to think of it schools have lots of steps
To climb them take vim, vigor and pep,
Vigor I have, lots of pep I'm sort on
Maybe there's elevators so I can take one.

I'm now in the classroom, where can the teacher be?
Oh h ere she comes now, Wow she's younger than me,
First to the Lab, then on to computers
Whoa!  I can't do this stuff, I need a tutor.

I looked all around to find a chair
Do they really expect me to fit in there,
I've had three kids, I haven't lost any weight
I haven't sat in one of those since 1958.

Time to go home, schools finally out
Wish I knew what these classes were about,
I really don't want to do this, my recliner looks good
Think I'll stay home and rest like an old woman should.

# New Knees Please

Remember Big Foot, he ain't got nothing on me
If my feet were as small as his I would be happy
They swell so bad I have to lay down
If I didn't, I'd look like a broke down Big Foot Clown.

You know my hand hurt bad the other day
And my friend told me to rub it with ___ Gay
What if I did as she said
I'd run my poor husband from our bed
Stinking up my house like a nursing home
Doesn't she realize I'll be there before long?

Whoa! I just stood up to answer the phone
And a pain shot up from my head to my groan
The pain was so bad it knocked me off my feet
So I crawled across the floor and into a seat
When I got up I started feeling fine
Until I realized I had fallen on these broke knees of mine.

You may think I'm joking but I'm not
In these knees lay the worst pain I got
I can walk across the room feeling good
Then turn around to walk and they feel like wood.

They want to replace both my knees
But I begged the doctor please, please, please.
You see I have a friend who had this done
She said it hurt so bad she could shoot them with a gun
And I believe she would have if she only had one.

You know people don't think you're hurtin'
When they see you rockin' like a chimp
They think you're being cool and trying to pimp.
But keep on living and you will see
Ain't nothing can bring you down like some broke down knees.

# Up and Down Blues
11/16/98

Have you ever just started to cry off and on?
No one's done nothin' to you
You don't know what is wrong.

One minute you're up, the next you're down
First there's a smile, then there's a frown
Let's see, no one has hurt my feelings
Maybe it's just life with which you're dealing.

Well I'm _ _, how old are you?
They say about fifty you start feeling blue,
I don't feel mistreated, I don't feel abused
Though sometimes in life you may feel misused.

Now pick up, shake it off and let's get going
If you don't before long, your age will start showing,
I'd rather tell you, don't guess my age
Cause if you guess higher, I might go into a rage.

I'm tired of feeling like this
Gotta get out of this slump
On your mark, get ready, set, jump
Gonna get myself over this hump.

I've evaluated everything
I feel better about myself
And where are those Blues
In the Blues house on the shelf.

# What's Happening
## 11/16/98

When I woke up this morning, my gown was all wet
I couldn't figure it out, I usually don't sweat,
The back of my neck was all clammy and cold
I've heard this happens when you start getting old.

Now that I think about it, just the other day
I was reading the paper and the words went away,
I held the paper out and I pulled it back in
They said it would happen but they didn't say when.

I get out of breath and I have to sit down
And yes I've stopped changing my furniture around,
You know things start changing the older you get
But I haven't expected it to arrive her yet.

Just as I'm cleaning and really get busy
I bend over to dust and I start to get dizzy,
Well it's time to stop cleaning, I'm done anyway
I'd rather go shopping for the rest of the day.

*Carol Hart-Parker*

## Arthur's House

I got up this morning with the best of intentions
Til my 'border showed up whose name I won't mention
I fed and massaged him as I've done before
But before the days done, I rub him some more.

You know this is ridiculous, most boarders pay
But this one lives on me from day to day
He leaves for awhile during the day
That's while I'm resting, so he can't get in my way.

But don't let me get busy, he's back bothering me again
Sometimes I feel he'll leave but I'd like to know when
He seems to think that he's my old friend
I wish he'd never bother me again
Please someone tell me what to do
He's as comfortable with me as I am an old shoe.

By now you've probably figured out who my old friend is
His first name is Arth, his last name is ritis
Well it's time to lay down again
I'll finally be rid of my old friend
But wait just a minute the other night it seems
Mr. Arthritis was involved in my dreams
Cause when I woke up, I was as tired as a dog and
Felt like I had been beat with a log.

Well another day I guess I'll get started
Seems my border and I will never be parted
I'm lucky Arthur didn't bring his family
To spend the rest of their lives with me.

# Wakin' Up Tired

I just woke up and I thank the Lord
But why in the world do I feel so tired?
I know I went to bed late last night
But I slept eight hours, I should feel alright.

When I lay flat, I have problems with my throat
So I sleep on four pillows so I don't choke,
Just when I get comfortable
In my back I get a pain
I guess I'll turn over on my stomach again.

When I sleep on my stomach
I feel like I'm sleeping on a ball
No, this position won't do at all,
I must figure out a good way to rest
So when I get up I will feel my best.

I know I don't do so much through the day
Then my tired aching bones won't have to pay,
It feels better to wake up all refreshed and new
So everyone around won't mind looking at you.

Are you tired when you awake?
With your head hurtin' and a body that aches,
Then take care of yourself and get plenty of rest
So your wonderful body won't be in a mess.

*Carol Hart-Parker*

## The Old Hand
11/12/98


My hand is hurting like never before
It feels like it's been smashed in a car door,
What is this brand new pain I feel
Wonder can it be cured with a pill.

My hand is throbbing, my thumb won't move
What in the world am I going to use,
All my control is in my right hand
If I try to use my left one, I'll drop this can.

If I don't cook again today this man is going to flip
I know I'll give him the can opener since his hand can grip,
Then he can cook while I wrap this thing
And lay back to see what pain tomorrow will bring.

# An All Day Job

It's an all day job taking care of me
I put drops in my eyes in order to see,
In order for these eyes to thrive
I have to tend them at least by five.

Just as I raise my arms to drop them in
Oh, goodness my shoulders hurtin' again,
I rubbed it last night with Alcohol
I just knew the pain wouldn't return at all.

I was making my bed-got a pain in my chest
I think today's the day I'm to take that test,
I hope the X-rays turn out alright
I can't stand another pill in my sight.

Well we won't talk about the rest of my day
All I'll say is that it didn't go my way,
Time for my bath, bedtime has arrived
You know what time I have to get up, five.

# Don't Go There, Remember!

There are many places in my house where,
For instance one is at my kitchen sink
When I was still at home with my sister and my brothers
I can clearly recall the voice of my mother saying...

"Carol, get those dishes done,"
Or, "No talking on the phone to anyone."
Boy, did I dislike being in that kitchen,
It was like I was on a cleaning mission.

Do you remember "Clean the table, wipe the chairs,
sweep the floor, or you'll go no where."
"Take the clothes from the washer, put um in the dryer,
before you fold them up, put some coal on the fire."

Wait a minute, I've confused the time
We didn't have dryers, we had clothes lines.
Hanging clothes out in early winter, some of us had that chore,
And when they were brought in they were as stiff as boards.

Ouch! I pricked my finger, now how did I do that?
Helping my Gramma stretch the lace curtains onto one of those racks.
Feed the chicken, pump some water, help me pick some sage.
Wow! I'd better end these poems before I tell my age.

Did you shake those rugs? Did you do it right?
Go to the porch and get the galvanized tub, you know it's Saturday night.
There is one thing toward which I still feel guilt,
And that is that I never helped my great aunt with her quilts.

# Mother—The Gift
May 9, 1999


There are many things in life
That should, but don't reap honor
I'm sure that you could thing of some
If through your mind you'd ponder.

I know of one that should be worldwide
And that's the love of a mother.

Truly, this woman is the gift of gifts.
Without her where would we be.
God molded and shaped and sculptured her
To bring forth you and me.

Some of us are blessed enough
To have our mothers for years.
Then some have to get go early
But we think of them with loving tears.

I pray with all the love of God
You have a caring, sharing and thoughtful mother
But if you are without children
You can be a mother to another.

Happy Mother's Day
Carol Hart-Parker

# W.W.J.D = Walk With Jesus Daily

Women in Christianity, now that's a thought
Just think of all the children these women of God have taught.
We should carry ourselves in an upright way
And always be careful of the things we say.

Do you go with your children to church or send them alone?
They need that supervision so from the church they will not roam.

I look at our children today, and wonder how they got that way.
Could it be we're losing control, they're grown before they're 10 years old.

Young mothers today have so much to deal with:
Drugs, weapons and corruption are real, not a myth.
God is so real, worshipping is such a treasure.
Why would one not come to this house that holds so many pleasures.

Let's not forget fathers, every household needs one
To instill good works before any harm's done.
But if in your house there's only a mother or a father
Guess who's your mate, Jesus, to him you're no bother.


Always carry this word with you wherever you go
It's meaning, means more than we'll ever know.
The word is Jesus           J= Jesus is just that good
                            E= Everyday give thanks
                            S= Saved is what we call can be
                            U= Utter prayers daily
                            S= Stay in church
You learn just how much your life is worth.

W.W.J.D. = Walk With Jesus Daily!!

*Carol Hart-Parker*

# • GUEST POETS •

*Carol Hart-Parker*

## Share of Light
### By Anthony Henderson

My Mon works at a shelter
I always go with her
The last Sunday in every month we share a meal
To the men at Broom field who things this is a big deal
I help serve the food
I always meet new friends
They are men without a home
But not without a heart
We prepare the food
The Food is very good
I didn't Mention
That they have a cool kitchen
It don't seem like much to us because we have been  blessed
But the men at the shelter think we are the best

*Carol Hart-Parker*

When some fellow yield's to temptation,
    and break's a conventional law,
We look for no good in his make-up.
But Lord, how we look for the flaw.

No one ask," who did the tempting?"
Nor allow's for the battle he's fought.
His name become's food for the jackass;
    the saint's who've never been caught.
I'am a sinner, O'Lord and I know it.
    I am weak and I blunder and fail.
I am tossed on life's stormy ocean,
    like a ship is caught in a gale.

I am willing to trust in they mercy.
    To keep the commandment's taught,
But deliver me Lord, from the judging,
Of saint's who've never been caught…

WRITTEN
BY:
JANICE
BANKS

*Carol Hart-Parker*

## WHO IS THIS AND WHO DRESSED HIM? ☺

### FROM BOBBY

Blue J.

Printed in the United States
4555